Disney · PIXAR

RATATOUILLE
(rat·a·too·ee)

WHAT'S COOKING?

A COOKBOOK FOR KIDS

Disney PRESS

New York

To all my young friends and future cooks of the world,

I have been cooking for over thirty years and I still cannot help but feel excited whenever food is discussed. It is the one subject whose history I find fascinating, and whose future I cannot wait to have unfolded.

I never had any formal culinary training. But growing up in a large family, I was always surrounded by food. I remember feeling comforted every time my mom served her favorite spaghetti dish and how much fun my brothers and I had fighting over the best parts of her roast chicken. I recall our many happy, chaotic gatherings during the holiday season and how everyone always seemed to gravitate toward the kitchen. And how many years later, when I decided to be a chef, I would call my big brother, Joseph, to help me with more difficult recipes. These days I enjoy cooking with my niece and nephews, and I am happy to make new and meaningful connections with them.

If you have never cooked before, don't be frightened. Cooking is supposed to be fun. It is also the perfect time to let your imagination run wild. Start with eggs! For me, eggs are the most versatile ingredient. Don't be sad if your first few attempts don't look quite like the pictures in the book. If it tastes good, you are doing great. I know your parents say this all the time, but it's true—"practice makes perfect"—especially in cooking.

After trying some of the basic recipes, I hope you will want to tackle the more difficult ones. Once we learn how to cook and know what goes into a dish, we make better and healthier decisions about the foods we eat. Cooking opens our minds to inspiration and possibilities.

So go on, put on your apron and pick up a spatula. Let's head to the kitchen, and, as my friend Chef Jacques Pépin always says, "Happy cooking!"

—Thomas Keller

Difficulty Level

★ Easy

★ ★ Medium

★ ★ ★ Master chef

Cooking Tips

◀ Before you get started, always wash your hands, put on an apron, and tie your hair back.

◀ Handle equipment and knives safely.

◀ Always ask a grown-up for help when using mixers, stoves, ovens, and sharp knives.

◀ Never touch a hot stove!

◀ Remember: always help clean up!

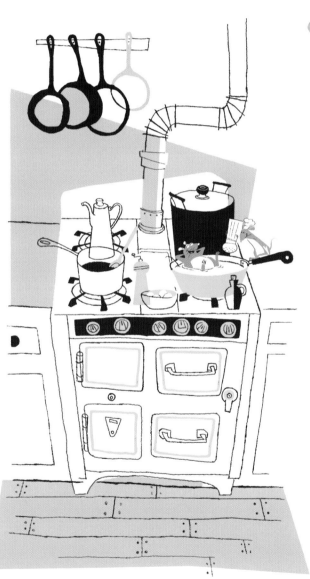

BON MATIN BREAKFAST

"Good food is like music you can taste, color you can smell."

COLETTE'S CREPES

INGREDIENTS

3 eggs	1 tablespoon sugar
1 ½ cups milk	¼ teaspoon salt
1 cup plus 2 tablespoons flour	2 tablespoons melted butter

1 Put all the ingredients in a blender in the order listed and blend until smooth. Remove the lid and scrape down the sides with a rubber spatula. Briefly blend the mixture again. Set the covered blender in the refrigerator for 30 minutes or even overnight.

2 When it's time to cook the crepes, use a paper towel to spread about 1 teaspoon of butter or vegetable oil in the bottom of an 8- or 9-inch shallow nonstick frying pan and place over medium heat. Blend the batter again to smooth it.

3 For the first crepe, pour ¼ to ⅓ cup of batter into a measuring cup to gauge how much to use. For the rest of the crepes, pour approximately that much batter right from the blender. Cook each crepe, following the steps at right.

4 Adjust the heat if they brown too quickly or too slowly. Makes 12 crepes.

CREPE FILLINGS

- ◀ Jam and cream cheese
- ◼ Mini chocolate chips and banana slices
- ▼ Nutella and ice cream

HOW **TO** COOK AND FLIP A CREPE

Pour the batter into your heated pan, well to one side. Immediately tilt and swirl the pan to evenly coat the bottom. This should take about 5 seconds.

Cook the crepe on the first side for about 45 seconds, then quickly flip it with a spatula and cook the other side for about half as long.

Grasping the pan securely, swiftly invert it so the cooked crepe will fall onto a large plate. Rub a little butter in the pan before cooking the next crepe.

OOH LA LA FRENCH TOAST

INGREDIENTS

- 4 eggs
- ½ cup milk
- 1 teaspoon vanilla extract
- 2 tablespoons butter or oil, for pan
- 8 slices dense bread

1 In a shallow bowl or pie plate, beat the eggs, then mix in the milk and vanilla extract.

2 Ask a grown-up to help you heat the butter in a frying pan over medium heat.

3 Soak the slices of bread in the egg mixture, turning once. They should be saturated but not falling apart.

4 Brown the bread in the skillet, turning once, about 2 to 3 minutes on each side. Serves 4.

Gusteau's Tip

The best French toast is made from the densest bread. Try challah, brioche, or sourdough!

REMY'S FAMOUS OMELETS

INGREDIENTS

2 eggs

1 teaspoon water

Pinch of salt

1 tablespoon butter

½ cup omelet filling (see below)

1 Crack the eggs into a small bowl. Add the water and salt and use a fork to beat the mixture until just blended.

2 Ask a grown-up to help you heat your frying pan on medium-high. Add the butter and spread it over the entire bottom of the pan as it melts.

3 Pour the beaten eggs into the pan and cook the omelet, following the step-by-step directions at right. Makes 1 omelet.

FAVORITE OMELET FILLINGS

- Steamed broccoli, grated cheddar cheese, and chopped cooked ham
- Fresh chopped herbs (such as chives, basil, or parsley) and cottage cheese
- Diced cooked chicken or turkey with diced green or red peppers
- Crisp bacon bits and shredded cheddar cheese

HOW TO COOK AN OMELET

Wait for the bottom of the eggs to cook a little, then gently push the eggs away from the edge. Tilt the pan so the uncooked egg runs into the spot you've created.

When the omelet surface looks almost cooked, add the filling over half of it. Slide a spatula under the plain half and fold it over the filling. The eggs should now be fully cooked.

To serve, tilt up the pan handle and slide the omelet out of the pan and onto your plate.

FRENCH BREAKFAST MUFFINS

★★

INGREDIENTS

2 cups flour

²/₃ cup sugar

2½ teaspoons baking powder

½ teaspoon salt

¼ teaspoon nutmeg

1 large egg

1 cup plus 2 tablespoons milk

6 tablespoons unsalted butter, melted and slightly cooled

1 teaspoon vanilla extract

CINNAMON-SUGAR COATING

2 tablespoons unsalted butter, melted and slightly cooled

½ cup sugar

½ teaspoon ground cinnamon

1. Heat the oven to 375°. Butter the cups of a 12-cup muffin pan and set aside.

2. Measure and whisk the flour, sugar, baking powder, salt, and nutmeg into a large mixing bowl.

3. In a separate bowl, whisk the egg until it's frothy. Blend in the milk, melted butter, and vanilla.

4. Make a well in the dry ingredients and pour in the liquid mixture. Using a wooden spoon, mix the batter until it's evenly blended. Then spoon it into the muffin cups, filling each about two-thirds full.

5. Bake the muffins on the center rack for about 20 minutes. Transfer the pan to a rack and let it cool for 5 minutes, then remove the muffins from the pan.

6. Meanwhile, prepare the topping by stirring the sugar and the cinnamon together in a bowl. In a separate bowl, melt the butter. Set both bowls next to the muffins.

7. Working with one muffin at a time, quickly dip the tops in the melted butter, and then in the cinnamon sugar, rolling each one to cover the entire muffin top. Makes 12 muffins.

HOW TO MAKE MUFFINS

To prevent sticking, rub a dab of butter in each muffin cup. Use a paper napkin so your hands don't get gooey.

Spoon the batter into the muffin cups. Fill each one about ²/₃ full.

Set the cinnamon sugar bowl and the melted butter bowl next to the muffins. Dip the muffins first in the butter, then in the cinnamon topping.

LET'S HAVE LUNCH

FROMAGE

"If you are what you eat, then I only want to eat the good stuff!"

GUSTEAU'S GRILLED CHEESE

INGREDIENTS

1 pat butter

2 slices bread

1 slice cheese

1 Ask a grown-up to help you melt the pat of butter in a frying pan.

2 Assemble the sandwich by placing the cheese between the two pieces of bread.

3 Carefully place the sandwich in the pan. Grill the sandwich on the first side for about 3 minutes, until golden brown. Then flip it with a spatula and grill it on the second side for another 3 minutes.

4 Using a spatula, transfer the sandwich from the pan to a plate, slice it in half, and serve. Makes 1.

Gusteau's Tip COOKIE CUTTER CHEESE TOASTS

Heat the oven or toaster oven to 350°. Place 2 slices of whole wheat bread on a cookie sheet or toaster-oven tray and top each with a slice of cheese. Cut out shapes using cookie cutters. Place the "cookies" in the oven and heat until the cheese melts. Serve warm or place in plastic bags when cool for a portable snack.

CROQUE MONSIEUR

INGREDIENTS

2 slices white bread

2 thin slices Swiss or cheddar cheese

2 thin slices deli ham

Cooking oil, for the pan

1 egg

½ tablespoon milk

Pinch of salt

¾ tablespoon butter

1 Layer 1 slice of bread with 1 slice of cheese followed by both slices of ham and the last piece of cheese. Add the second piece of bread.

2 Use a piece of paper towel to rub an unheated heavy skillet with a little cooking oil. Ask a grown-up to help you place the skillet over moderate heat.

3 As the skillet heats, whisk the egg, milk, and salt in a shallow bowl until frothy.

4 Melt the butter in the pan. As it melts, dip one side of the sandwich in the egg batter and then dip the other side.

5 Immediately place the sandwich in the pan. Grill the sandwich on the first side for about 3 minutes, until golden brown. Then flip it with a spatula and grill it on the second side for another 3 minutes.

6 Using a spatula, transfer the sandwich from the pan to a plate, slice it in half, and serve. Makes 1 sandwich.

QUICHE LORRAINE

★ ★

INGREDIENTS

- 1 pie crust in a 9-inch pie pan
- 3 eggs
- 1 ⅓ cups half-and-half or whole milk
- ½ teaspoon salt
- ¼ teaspoon black pepper
- 4 strips cooked bacon
- 2 cups grated cheese (your favorite kind, or Lorraine Swiss cheese)

1 Preheat the oven to 375°. Whisk the eggs, half-and-half or milk, salt, and pepper in a large bowl.

2 Crumble the bacon and sprinkle it in the pie shell. Sprinkle on about half of the grated cheese.

3 Ladle the egg mixture over the filling, then sprinkle on the remaining cheese.

4 Bake at 375° on the center oven rack until slightly puffy and golden brown, about 40 to 45 minutes. Serve warm, at room temperature, or cold. Makes 8 servings.

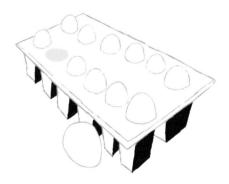

EASY FAUX ESCARGOTS

INGREDIENTS

Mayonnaise or whipped cream cheese

Large tortilla (square, if available)

Lettuce or baby spinach

Sliced deli meat of your choice

Sliced cheese of your choice

Gherkin pickles

Chives

1 If necessary, trim the rounded edges of the tortilla to make it square, then spread a thin layer of the mayonnaise or cream cheese on top.

2 Layer on the lettuce or spinach, then the meat and cheese and roll it up tightly.

3 With the seam on the bottom, slice the tortilla into 2-inch-wide pinwheels. For the heads, cut a pickle in half at an angle. Poke 2 small holes in the uncut end and stick pieces of chive with knots at one end in each hole for antennae.

4 Slip each pickle half under the edge of a pinwheel, securing them together with a toothpick if necessary. Makes 4 to 6 pinwheel sandwiches.

CRAZY CHEESE STRAWS

INGREDIENTS

1 ½ cups flour

6 tablespoons butter, softened

2 cups grated cheddar cheese

1 ½ cups grated Parmesan and/or Romano cheese

1 egg

¼ cup milk

1 Heat the oven to 400°. Grease 2 baking sheets.

2 Have a grown-up help you place the flour, butter, and cheeses in a food processor fitted with a metal blade. Pulse for about 1 minute, until the butter and cheese are evenly distributed in the flour. Add the egg and pulse until it's incorporated. With the processor running, pour the milk though the feed tube and blend until the dough forms a ball (about 1 minute). If the dough feels sticky, add a bit more Parmesan or Romano.

3 Place half of the dough on a floured work surface. With a rolling pin, roll out the dough until it's roughly ⅛-inch thick and then trim it into a rectangle. Next, cut the pastry into strips about 4 inches long and ½-inch wide. Twist the strips and place them on a baking sheet, 2 inches apart. Repeat the process until all the dough has been used.

4 Bake the sticks for 8 to 10 minutes, until they're lightly browned. Store them in an airtight container for up to 1 week. Makes about 60 straws.

CHEESE FONDUE

INGREDIENTS

12 ounces Swiss cheese (or cheddar, Gruyère, or a combination)

4 tablespoons flour

¼ teaspoon paprika

¼ teaspoon ground nutmeg

1 garlic clove

3 tablespoons butter

2 ¼ to 2 ½ cups milk

Juice from a lemon

Salt and pepper to taste

Dippers, such as French bread, carrots, peppers, broccoli, or cherry tomatoes

1 First, grate the cheese into a bowl. Toss with 1 tablespoon of the flour. Set aside.

2 In a separate bowl, stir together the remaining 3 tablespoons of flour, paprika, and nutmeg.

3 Peel the garlic clove. Next, cut the clove in half and rub the cut sides on the inside of a medium-size saucepan until the bottom and sides are completely seasoned.

4 Melt the butter in the pan over medium-low heat and stir in the flour mixture until it is smooth. This is called a roux (pronounced *roo*) and serves as the base that will help the fondue thicken. Add the milk, 1 cup at a time, and stir constantly until the sauce is creamy and warm.

5 Next, add the grated cheese by the handful, stirring well after each addition. Continue until the cheese is used up, and the sauce is thoroughly combined. Once the cheese has melted, stir in the lemon juice and salt and pepper to taste.

6 Meanwhile, prepare the dippers for the fondue. Cut the bread into cubes. Cut the vegetables into bite-size pieces and steam for a few minutes, if desired, to bring out the flavor.

7 Arrange the vegetables on a large platter and the bread cubes in a basket or bowl. Pour the fondue into a fondue pot. Invite everyone to spear the bread or vegetables on their fondue forks, then dip them into the cheesy sauce. Serves 8 people as an appetizer or 4 as a main course.

This milk-based fondue is milder than the traditional Swiss cheese fondue, which contains wine. If you don't like the strong taste of Swiss, substitute cheddar or a mixture of cheddar and Swiss.

FRENCH BREAD

SOUP DU JOUR

MMM...SALADS

"You must be imaginative, strong-hearted;
you must try things that may not work.
What I say is true—anyone can cook, but
only the fearless can be great!"

A CLASSIC BAGUETTE

INGREDIENTS

1 tablespoon active dry yeast

1½ cups warm water

3¾ to 4½ cups flour

1½ teaspoons salt

2 tablespoons cornmeal

1 In a small bowl, dissolve the yeast in ½ cup of the water. Pour the remaining water into a large bowl and add 1 cup of the flour and the salt. Add the yeast mixture and enough flour to form a soft dough. Turn the dough out onto a lightly floured surface and knead for 10 minutes.

2 Grease a large bowl with oil and drop the dough in, turning to coat the top. Cover with plastic wrap or a damp cloth and let it rise in a draft-free area for 2 hours, or until the dough doubles in size.

3 Punch the dough down and divide it in half. On a lightly floured surface, knead each half several times and roll into a snake. Pinch out any air bubbles, then place the snakes on a cookie sheet coated with the cornmeal. Cover and let rise until doubled, about 1 hour.

4 Heat the oven to 425°. Place a metal pan on the bottom rack and pour 1 cup of hot water into the pan (this will create the steam to give your bread a crunchy crust). Using a sharp knife make four diagonal ¼-inch cuts in the top of the loaves. Place the loaves in the oven. Bake for 20 to 25 minutes. Remove from the oven and cool. These loaves are best eaten the day they are made, or frozen. Makes 2 loaves.

Gusteau's Tip

Classic French bread—or the baguette—bakes in a long, narrow loaf pan, which is available at kitchen supply stores. If you don't have one, you can get almost the same crisp brown crust and light interior by baking the bread on a cookie sheet.

VICHYSSOISE

INGREDIENTS

5 cups peeled, chopped all-purpose potatoes

3 cups thinly sliced leeks (use the white and 2 inches of the green)

1 ²/₃ cups chicken broth

5 cups water

1 teaspoon salt

¹/₂ teaspoon white pepper

¹/₂ cup heavy cream

Chopped chives (optional)

1 In a soup pot, add the potatoes, leeks, broth, water, salt, and pepper. Ask a grown-up to help you turn the stove to simmer, and cook for 1 hour.

2 In batches, puree the soup and pour it into a large bowl. Stir in the cream. Serve warm or cold. Makes 6 to 8 servings.

Gusteau's Tip

Be sure you wash the leeks thoroughly to remove any sand.

CHEF'S SALAD

★ ★ ★

INGREDIENTS

2 to 4 eggs

2 slices whole wheat bread

2 tablespoons butter

3/4 teaspoon garlic powder

1 head romaine lettuce

1 large carrot

1 medium-size cucumber

1 red or green pepper

A handful of cherry tomatoes

1/2 pound cubed cooked ham or chicken breast

1/4 pound cubed Swiss cheese

1 Begin by making the toppings for this chef's salad. For hard-boiled eggs, place two to four eggs in a heavy saucepan and cover with cold water. Boil for 1 minute, then turn off the heat. Cover and let sit for 15 minutes in the hot water. Next, drain the hot water and run cold water over the eggs. Roll each egg gently to crack the shell, then peel. Rinse well, then slice into four wedges. For easy peeling, work under a running tap or in a bowl of water.

2 For garlic croutons, cut two slices of whole wheat bread into sixteen squares each. In a small microwave-safe bowl, melt the butter on high (about 40 seconds). Stir in 1/4 teaspoon of the garlic powder and toss in the bread cubes. Arrange the cubes in a single layer on a baking sheet or toaster-oven tray. Broil for 1 to 2 minutes, checking frequently to prevent burning. Turn and brown the other side. Transfer to a paper towel to drain and cool.

3 To prepare the lettuce, cut 1 1/2 inches off the stem end of the romaine head and discard. Break the leaves off and wash in cold water. Place in a salad spinner and spin until dry (or pat dry with paper towels). Break the leaves into bite-size pieces and place in a large salad bowl.

4 To prepare the vegetables, peel and grate the carrot; wash, peel, and slice the cucumber; and wash and cut the pepper into strips with a knife or into shapes with a mini cookie cutter. Wash the tomatoes and remove the stems. Place the ham or chicken, cheese, croutons, and hard-boiled eggs in bowls and serve with dressing.

5 Next, hand everyone a plate and let them assemble their own salad. Pour salad dressing over the salad or serve it on the side for dipping. Serves 4.

SALAD NICOISE

INGREDIENTS

1 head of romaine lettuce

1 can white tuna, drained

10 cherry tomatoes

2 hard-boiled eggs

Olives, such as Nicoise

Green beans, steamed

Anchovies (optional)

Dijon vinaigrette dressing (below)

1 To prepare the lettuce, cut 1½ inches off the stem end of the romaine head and discard. Break the leaves off and wash in cold water. Place in a salad spinner and spin until dry (or pat dry with paper towels). Arrange on individual salad plates as shown.

2 Next, prepare the toppings for the salad. Peel the eggs and slice each one into four wedges. Wash the tomatoes and cut in half. Arrange chunks of the tuna, hard-boiled eggs, tomatoes, olives, and green beans on top of the lettuce. Add the anchovies, if you're feeling adventurous.

3 Pour the Dijon vinaigrette over the salad or serve it on the side for dipping. Serves 4.

DIJON VINAIGRETTE

INGREDIENTS

⅓ cup red wine vinegar

½ cup olive oil

½ cup vegetable oil

1 crushed garlic clove

½ teaspoon thyme

2 teaspoons Dijon mustard

¼ teaspoon salt

⅛ teaspoon coarse black pepper

1 Combine all the ingredients in a clean jar with a tight-fitting lid. Shake well. Makes 1⅓ cups.

DINNER IS SERVED!

"In every dish, Chef Gusteau
always has something
unexpected."

GUSTEAU'S RATATOUILLE

INGREDIENTS

1 large eggplant, cubed

¹/₄ to ¹/₃ cup olive oil

1 onion, thinly sliced

1 red or green pepper, chopped

2 to 4 crushed garlic cloves

4 small zucchini, chopped

4 tomatoes, chopped

Salt and pepper to taste

¹/₃ cup chopped fresh basil

Parmesan cheese

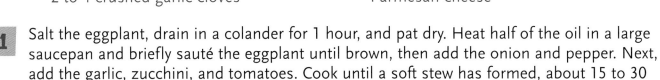

★ ★ ★

1 Salt the eggplant, drain in a colander for 1 hour, and pat dry. Heat half of the oil in a large saucepan and briefly sauté the eggplant until brown, then add the onion and pepper. Next, add the garlic, zucchini, and tomatoes. Cook until a soft stew has formed, about 15 to 30 minutes.

2 Add the salt, pepper, and basil. Sprinkle with the cheese and serve. You can freeze leftovers. Serves 4.

Gusteau's Tip

This French Mediterranean stew is meant to be served over rice.

LINGUINI ALFREDO WITH PEAS

INGREDIENTS

1 pound linguini

1 cup frozen petite peas

4 tablespoons butter

1 cup heavy cream

$^2/_3$ cup freshly grated Parmesan cheese

$^1/_2$ teaspoon salt

Pinch of ground nutmeg

1 Boil the linguini according to the directions on the package. In the last minute of boiling, add the frozen peas. Strain the cooked pasta and peas. Set aside.

2 To prepare the Alfredo sauce, bring the butter and cream to a boil and immediately lower the heat so the mixture gently simmers. Cook the sauce, stirring occasionally, for about 4 minutes or until it leaves a thick coating on the spoon. Stir in the grated cheese, salt, and nutmeg.

3 Dish out the cooked linguini and peas. Top with the Alfredo sauce. Serves 4.

C'EST MAGNIFIQUE SALMON

INGREDIENTS

4 six-ounce salmon steaks, 1 inch thick

Half a lemon

QUICK DILL SAUCE

1/2 cup sour cream

1/4 cup mayonnaise

2 tablespoons milk

1 1/2 teaspoons dill

1 small garlic clove, crushed

Salt and pepper

1 In a small bowl, whisk the sour cream, mayonnaise, and milk until creamy. Add the dill, garlic, and salt and pepper to taste. Stir well; set aside.

2 Preheat your broiler or grill. Rinse the salmon steaks and pat them dry. Squeeze the lemon over the steaks and sprinkle with salt and pepper.

3 Broil or grill the steaks 3 inches from the heat for 8 to 10 minutes, or until the fish has turned from a bright pink to a pale orange. Serve with the dill sauce. Serves 4 to 6.

Gusteau's Tip

Whether you're shopping at your local grocer's or a fish market, always look for the freshest fish. It should have a firm, moist flesh and a sweet smell—never a fishy smell, which is a sure sign of aging.

REMY'S MACARONI AND CHEESE

INGREDIENTS

1 pound elbow macaroni, cooked according to package directions

Butter for greasing the dish

3 cups half-and-half or whole milk

12 to 18 slices American or cheddar cheese

12 Ritz crackers

Salt, pepper, and paprika to taste

1 Heat the oven to 350° and grease a 13 x 9 inch baking pan or a large casserole dish.

2 Spoon a third of the cooked macaroni into the pan, then pour in 1 cup of the half-and-half or milk and cover everything with 4 to 6 slices of the cheese. Add two more layers of pasta, half-and-half or milk, and cheese.

3 Place the crackers in a ziplock bag and crush. Add the salt, pepper, and paprika, then sprinkle the crumbs on top of the pasta and cheese. Bake until bubbly, about 35 to 45 minutes. Makes 6 to 8 servings.

46

PIZZA RATS

INGREDIENTS

Tomato sauce

English muffins

Black olives

Scallions

Cheese sticks or slices

1 Heat a toaster oven to 350°. Using a pizza slicer, cut an English muffin half into a triangle, as shown. Spread a tablespoon of tomato sauce onto the wedge.

2 Set round olive slices in place for eyes and a nose. Add round slices of green onion for pupils and lay strips of cheese (we used a pulled-apart cheese stick) across the muffin for the rat's fur.

3 Bake for about 10 minutes, or until the cheese is melted and the muffin is toasty.

OVEN-BAKED FRENCH FRIES

INGREDIENTS

4 medium Idaho potatoes

¼ cup olive oil

Salt to taste

1 Heat the oven to 425°. Peel the potatoes and slice them into about 10 wedges. Dry off any excess starch with paper towels.

2 In a baking dish, toss the potatoes with the oil to coat. Bake for 25 minutes, turning at least once. Add salt to taste. Makes 4 servings.

DELIGHTFUL DESSERTS

"Mmm...
flour, eggs, sugar..."

INGREDIENTS

1 baked 13 x 9 x 2 inch cake

2 to 2½ cups white frosting

Pale green sour strips or fruit leather

Kids' kitchen utensils (wooden spoon or whisk)

Blue decorator's icing

1 Set the baked cake on a serving platter. Cut away the upper corners of the cake to form an apron shape. Frost the cake with the white frosting. Stick the sour strips into the top of the cake to form the neck strap and into the sides of the cake to form the apron strings.

2 Stick the kids' cooking utensils into the apron in the lower left side of the cake. Using the blue decorator's icing and a writing tip, outline the shape of the pocket, with the utensils poking out of the top. Form the pocket with a mound of decorator's icing, smooth it out well, and add a sour strip. Use the icing to write "What's Cooking?" on the apron. Serves 10 to 12.

DJANGO'S DIRT CAKE

INGREDIENTS

1 baked 13 x 9 x 2 inch cake

1 dome cake (baked in a 2-quart bowl)

3 to 4 cups chocolate frosting

2 to 3 cups crushed chocolate cookies (we combined chocolate graham crackers, fudge cookies, and chocolate wafer cookies)

Gummy worms

Plastic rats, washed and dried

1. Place the dome cake on the rectangular cake, as shown at right, securing with frosting. Cover the cakes with the frosting, then sprinkle on the cookie crumbs.

2. Decorate with the gummy worms and plastic rats. (For safety, remove the toys before serving.) Serves 12 to 14.

Gusteau's Tip   HOW TO BAKE A DOME CAKE

For a dome-shaped cake, bake your cake batter in a 1 1/2 quart ovenproof bowl (stainless steel or Pyrex) for 45 to 55 minutes.

CHERRY CHEESECAKES

INGREDIENTS

1 ¼ cups chocolate graham cracker crumbs

½ cup sugar, divided

⅓ cup butter or margarine, melted

12 ounces cream cheese, softened

2 teaspoons grated lemon peel

2 teaspoons vanilla extract

2 cups whipped topping

1 20-ounce can cherry pie filling

1 In a medium mixing bowl, combine the graham cracker crumbs, ¼ cup of the sugar, and the butter or margarine, mixing well. Firmly press the crumb mixture into the bottom of a muffin pan or 9 x 9 x 2 inch baking pan. Place the pan in the refrigerator to chill while you make the cheesecake filling.

2 In a large bowl, combine the cream cheese, lemon peel, vanilla extract, and the remaining ¼ cup of sugar. Beat with an electric mixer until light and fluffy, about 2 minutes. Fold in the whipped topping, then spread the mixture onto the chilled crust.

3 Spread the cherry pie filling over the cheese mixture. Chill the cheesecake in the refrigerator until ready to serve. Makes 9 servings.

Gusteau's Tip

This easy, no-bake treat combines the flavors of chocolate, cherries, and cheesecake, so it's bound to be a family favorite. Make it as an after-school cooking project and serve it for dessert at dinnertime.

CHOCOLATE BOUCHONS

BY THOMAS KELLER

★ ★ ★

INGREDIENTS

3 ½ ounces (¾ cup) all-purpose flour

1 cup unsweetened cocoa powder

1 teaspoon kosher salt

3 large eggs

¾ cup plus 2 tablespoons granulated sugar

½ teaspoon vanilla extract

3 sticks (12 ounces) unsalted butter, melted and just slightly warm

6 ounces semisweet chocolate chips

Confectioners' sugar

1 Preheat the oven to 350°. Place muffin liners in a 12-cup muffin pan. Set aside.

2 Sift the flour, cocoa powder, and salt into a large bowl and set aside.

3 In another large bowl, mix together the eggs and sugar with a handheld mixer on medium speed for about 3 minutes, or until very pale in color. Mix in the vanilla. On low speed, add about ⅓ of the dry ingredients, then ⅓ of the butter, and continue alternating with the remaining flour and butter. Add the chocolate and mix to combine. (The batter can be refrigerated for up to a day.)

4 Fill each muffin cup about ⅔ full. Place in the oven and bake for 20 to 25 minutes. When the tops look shiny and set (like a brownie), test one cake with a toothpick: it should come out clean but not dry.

5 Transfer the bouchons in their liners to a cooling rack. After a couple of minutes, invert the bouchons and let them cool upside down in their liners; then lift off the liners. (The bouchons are best eaten the day they are baked.)

6 Invert the bouchons and dust them with confectioners' sugar. Serve with ice cream, if desired. Makes 12 servings.

CHOCOLATE RATS

INGREDIENTS

1 cup semisweet chocolate chips

1 tablespoon vegetable shortening

48 dried apricots

Wooden skewers

48 M&M'S Minis

Black shoestring licorice (whiskers)

24 dry-roasted peanut halves (ears)

1 Place the chocolate chips and shortening in a microwave-safe bowl and microwave on high for 1 minute. Stir and microwave for 1 minute more. Stir until smooth.

2 For each rat, press together 2 dried apricots, making a small point for the rat's nose, and thread them onto a skewer. Dip them in the melted chocolate and place on a waxed-paper–lined baking sheet. Use a second skewer to push the rat off the first skewer; use your fingertip to cover the hole left behind with chocolate.

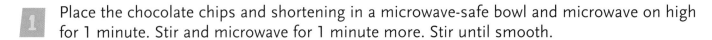

3 Add M&M'S Minis for the eyes, shoestring licorice for the whiskers, Tootsie Rolls or any other pliable candy, such as Starburst or soft taffy, for the tail, and peanuts for the ears (we broke each peanut half in half again). Refrigerate until hardened. Makes 24.

EIFFEL TOWER COOKIE SUNDAE

INGREDIENTS

Sugar wafers

White frosting

Ice cream (optional)

Chocolate sauce (optional)

1 Build an Eiffel Tower on your plate using sugar wafers as your building blocks and frosting as your cement. You will need to cut some cookies into smaller shapes so your tower stands.

2 Make a French flag by drawing one on paper using markers or crayons, then cut it out, and tape or glue it to a whole or a half toothpick depending on how tall you want it to stand. Add the flag to the top of the tower.

3 Serve with a scoop of ice cream and chocolate sauce, if desired.

ACKNOWLEDGMENTS:
This book would not have been possible without the talented *FamilyFun* magazine staff,
who edited the recipes which originally ran in the magazine.
We'd like to particularly thank Deanna F. Cook
(Creative Development Director of *FamilyFun* magazine)
for her help with this project.

Designed by Impress: Pam Glaven and Hans Teenma
Cover Design: Winnie Ho and Impress
Photography by Joanne Schmaltz
except as follows—Shaffer/Smith Photography: 7, 11 (process steps);
John Gruen: 13; Deborah Jones: 59; Jacqueline Hopkins: 60
Food Styling by Edwina Stevenson
except as follows—Marie Pirano: 7, 11 (process steps), 13; Karen Quatsoe and Lee Levin: 60

Chocolate Bouchons recipe excerpted from Bouchon, Copyright 2004 © by Thomas Keller
Photographs copyright 2004 © by Deborah Jones. Used by permission of Artisan,
a division of Workman Publishing Co., Inc. New York. All Rights Reserved.

White ceramics on 9 (small oval platter), 17, 21, 23, 33 (plate only), 35, 36,
40, 43, 45, 49, 55 (plate in background), 57, 61, 62 are by VIETRI.
For more information and preferred stores, please visit www.vietri.com

FamilyFun is a division of the Walt Disney Publishing Group. To order a subscription, call-800-289-4849.

ISBN-13: 978-14231-0540-4
ISBN-10: 1-4231-0540-0

Library of Congress Cataloging-in-Publication Data on file.
First Edition
10 9 8 7 6 5 4 3 2 1